Donovan McNabb

by Michael Sandler

Consultant: Norries Wilson
Head Football Coach, Columbia University

BEARPORT
PUBLISHING

New York, New York

Credits

Cover and Title Page, © Hunter Martin/WireImage/Newscom; 4, © Gary Bogdon/MCT/
Landov; 5, © AP Images/Mark Lennihan; 6, © Reuters/Landov; 7, © Icon Sports Media/
newscom; 8, Courtesy of the McNabb family; 9, Courtesy of the McNabb family; 10, Courtesy
of the McNabb family; 11, © James Prisching/MCT/Landov; 12, © Rick Stewart/Getty
Images; 13, © Michael Bush/UPI/Landov; 14, © Tom Mihalek/AFP/Getty Images; 15, © John
Angelillo/UPI/Landov; 16, © AP Images/Rusty Kennedy; 17, © Jim Rogash/NFL/Getty Images;
18, Courtesy of the McNabb family; 19, Courtesy of the Philadelphia Eagles; 20, © AP Images/
H. Rumph Jr; 21, © AP Images/Matt Rourke; 22, © Molly Riley/Reuters/Landov; 22Logo, ©
PRNewsFoto/The Philadelphia Eagles.

Publisher: Kenn Goin
Senior Editor: Lisa Wiseman
Creative Director: Spencer Brinker
Photo Researcher: Omni-Photo Communications, Inc.
Design: Dawn Beard Creative

Library of Congress Cataloging-in-Publication Data

Sandler, Michael, 1965-
  Donovan McNabb / by Michael Sandler ; consultant, Norries Wilson.
      p. cm. — (Football heroes making a difference)
  Includes bibliographical references and index.
  ISBN-13: 978-1-59716-772-7 (library binding)
  ISBN-10: 1-59716-772-X (library binding)
  1. McNabb, Donovan—Juvenile literature. 2. Football players—United States—Biography—
Juvenile literature. 3. Quarterbacks (Football)—Biography—Juvenile literature. I. Wilson,
Norries. II. Title.
  GV939.M38S35 2009
  796.332092—dc22
  [B]
                                            2008040262

For more information, write to Bearport Publishing Company, Inc., 101 Fifth Avenue, Suite 6R,
New York, New York 10003. Printed in the United States of America in North
Mankato, Minnesota.

042011
040111CGC

10 9 8 7 6 5 4 3

CONTENTS

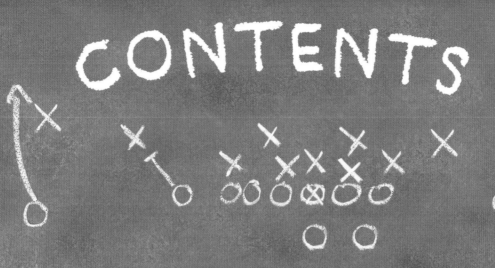

Hearing the Boos

Donovan McNabb was so excited! One of his dreams was about to come true. In just a few minutes he was going to be **drafted** by an **NFL** team! Which one would he play for?

Soon he had the answer—the Philadelphia Eagles. Donovan was thrilled, but Philly fans weren't happy. They had wanted a different player. The sound of their booing was deafening. Donovan was shocked, but he made himself a promise: *I'll show these fans that I'm the right pick.*

During the 1999 draft, Eagles fans had wanted the team to choose running back Ricky Williams instead of Donovan. Ricky ended up with the New Orleans Saints.

Donovan holds up his Eagles jersey while posing with friends and family.

Donovan was the second player chosen in the 1999 NFL draft.

The Right Choice

To change people's minds, Donovan knew he had to deliver wins. His chance came during his first professional start in November 1999. Donovan showed off a special talent that few quarterbacks have—the ability to run with the ball. He carried it nine times as the Eagles beat the Washington Redskins, 35-28.

The following season, Philadelphia fans finally realized how wrong they had been about Donovan. The once-unwanted quarterback led the Eagles to one win after another. Philadelphia finished with an 11-5 record and made it into the second round of the playoffs.

No other Eagles quarterback had won his first start as a rookie in 25 years.

Donovan's passing was as good as his running. In a 38-10 win against the Atlanta Falcons, he threw for over 300 yards (274 m).

In 2000, Donovan was runner-up as the NFL's **MVP**. He came in second to St. Louis Rams **running back** Marshall Faulk.

A New Game

If it wasn't for a **persistent** coach, Donovan might never have become a quarterback. While growing up in Dolton, Illinois, Donovan was a big sports fan. His bedroom walls were covered with pictures of athletes. What was his favorite game? Basketball! It wasn't until seventh grade that he decided to give football a try.

When Donovan asked his parents for permission to join a team, his mom said no. She thought football was too dangerous. Then the team's coach called her. He promised her that Donovan wouldn't get hurt. She soon changed her mind, and Donovan began playing football.

Donovan (second row, second from the right) also played on a Little League baseball team, the Dolton Leafs.

Donovan (far right) with his family in Dolton, Illinois, a suburb of Chicago

In high school, Donovan played both basketball and football. One of his teammates on the basketball team was Antoine Walker, the future **NBA** star who won a championship with the Miami Heat.

High School Star

It didn't take Donovan long to learn the game of football. At Mt. Carmel High School, he became the team's star quarterback. His throwing arm was strong, but his legs were just as **vital**. If there was no one to pass the ball to, Donovan would scramble away and gain yards by running.

Equally important was his brain. Donovan was smart. He always seemed to make the right play. By senior year, colleges were lining up to **recruit** him. Donovan chose Syracuse University.

Donovan (#1) was chosen as an All-American high school quarterback. This meant that he was one of the best athletes in the country.

Donovan (#1) leads his high school team.

As a **sophomore** in 1991, Donovan helped Mt. Carmel win an Illinois state championship.

Super at Syracuse

At Syracuse, Donovan quickly became team leader. "On game day," said the **offensive coach**, "he's one of those guys the other players feel **confident** about, knowing he'll do what's right."

Syracuse won 35 of 49 games and three **Big East** championships with Donovan playing quarterback. Syracuse head coach Paul Pasqualoni knew he'd go on to be a great **pro**—even when he got booed on draft day. "They don't know it yet," said Pasqualoni, "but they're going to love him in Philadelphia."

As a **freshman**, Donovan threw a 96-yard (88-m) pass, the longest in Syracuse history.

During his senior year, Donovan (#5) led Syracuse to an Orange Bowl appearance against the University of Florida.

13

Winning Fans in Philadelphia

Pasqualoni was right. By the end of the 2000 season, they did love Donovan in Philadelphia. The love grew stronger when Donovan led the team into three straight **NFC Championship Games** and, finally, after the 2004 season, to Super Bowl XXXIX (39).

It wasn't just the winning that made fans **appreciate** their quarterback; it was the toughness Donovan showed. In a game against the Arizona Cardinals, he hurt his ankle but refused to stop playing. Four touchdown passes later, the Eagles had a win. Donovan learned later that his ankle was broken.

Despite breaking his ankle on the game's third play, Donovan (#5) completed 20 of 25 passes in the 2002 win against the Arizona Cardinals.

Donovan tries to escape from Rosevelt Colvin of the New England Patriots during Super Bowl XXXIX (39).

In Super Bowl XXXIX (39), the Eagles lost a close, hard-fought game to the New England Patriots, 24–21.

Fighting Diabetes

Donovan knows that staying healthy is a key to his success. In 2005 and 2007, he struggled with injuries. The Eagles missed the playoffs both seasons.

Donovan also knows that good health is important for everyone, not just athletes. He was filled with sadness when his grandmother died from a disease called diabetes. When his father got sick with the same illness, Donovan decided to see what he could do to help fight it.

In 2000, he started the Donovan McNabb **Foundation**. This group has raised hundreds of thousands of dollars for the **American Diabetes Association** (ADA).

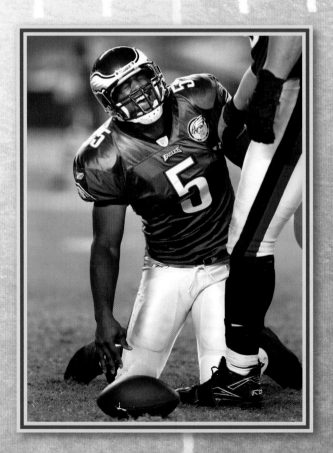

Donovan in pain after getting sacked by the Chicago Bears in 2007

Here, Donovan announces a donation of one million cans of Campbell's Chunky Soup to food banks across the United States. (handwritten on check)

Campbell's CHUNKY TACKLING HUNGER NFL

January 3-1, 20 07

TO **Food Banks Nationwide** 1,000,000

One million cans of Chunky soup

Chunky/NFL
FOR Tackling Hunger program

Campbell Soup Company

10185652:4589:15

Donovan is a national spokesperson for the ADA. He also works with many other groups and companies that help people in need. Here, Donovan announces a donation of one million cans of Campbell's Chunky Soup to food banks across the United States.

Diabetes is a disease that affects the way the body processes sugar. People who have this disease may have too much sugar in their blood. There is no cure, but there are treatments that help people with diabetes live normal lives.

Helping Kids

With money from Donovan's foundation, the ADA **sponsors** the Donovan McNabb Camp in Green Lake, Pennsylvania. Every summer, over 100 kids with diabetes are invited to spend a week at the camp. They swim, play sports, and have a good time there. The high point of the week for most of them is meeting the star Philadelphia quarterback.

For Donovan, the high point is seeing the kids have fun. "I want them to know life isn't over because you have diabetes," he says. "You can still play basketball. You can play tennis. You can be whatever it is you strive to be."

Donovan plays volleyball with some campers.

Over 23 million American kids and adults are living with diabetes.

Since 2003, Donovan has participated in the "NFL Take a Player to School" event. On this day, Donovan visits a school and promotes after-school activities and encourages students to finish their education.

19

Earning Cheers, Saving Lives

Today Donovan is one of Philadelphia's best-loved athletes. Once in a while, though, he still hears booing. Philly fans are tough. If he makes a bad play, they let him know.

Donovan doesn't get upset, though. He knows if he plays hard, the boos will turn to cheers. Donovan also knows something else: football isn't his most important job. If he can save one life by teaching people about diabetes, it means more than any pass he will ever throw.

A healthy Donovan during preseason practice in 2008

On June 4, 2008, Donovan and his teammates helped build a playground at the William Bryant Academic Plus School in Philadelphia.

In 2008, Donovan began his 10th season as the Eagles' starting quarterback.

The Donovan File

Donovan is a football hero on and off the field. Here are some highlights.

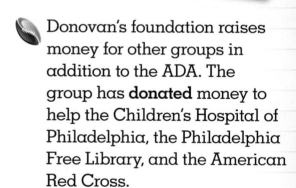

- At Syracuse University, Donovan played on the basketball team during his freshman and sophomore years. Then he left the team to focus completely on football.

- Donovan was named the 2004 NFC Offensive Player of the Year. He also has made the NFC Pro Bowl team five times.

- Donovan's foundation holds an annual free football **clinic.** Hundreds of kids, ages 10 to 14, get to practice their football skills with Donovan and other NFL players and coaches.

- Donovan's foundation raises money for other groups in addition to the ADA. The group has **donated** money to help the Children's Hospital of Philadelphia, the Philadelphia Free Library, and the American Red Cross.

- Donovan has also given money to Syracuse University. He looks back fondly on his experience there. "I came to Syracuse as a young boy, and I left as a man," he said. "It was the most enjoyable time of my life."

Glossary

American Diabetes Association
(uh-MER-uh-kuhn *dye*-uh-BEE-teez
uh-*soh*-see-AY-shuhn) a group that
tries to find treatments and cures for
diabetes, raise awareness about the
disease, and help improve the lives of
people who suffer from it

appreciate (uh-PREE-shee-*ate*) to
like and respect; to be happy to have
something

Big East (BIG EEST) a group of college
teams, including Syracuse University,
that play games against one another;
an athletic conference

clinic (KLIN-ik) a place where kids can
go to practice their football skills and
learn more about the sport

confident (KON-fuh-duhnt) to believe
in one's abilities

donated (DOH-nate-id) gave something
as a gift

drafted (DRAFT-id) picked after college
to play for an NFL team

foundation (foun-DAY-shuhn) an
organization that supports or gives
money to worthwhile causes

freshman (FRESH-muhn) a person in his
or her first year of high school or college

MVP (EM-VEE-PEE) the most valuable
player in a game or a season

NBA (EN-BEE-AY) the National
Basketball Association

NFC Championship Games
(EN-EFF-SEE CHAM-pee-uhn-*ship*
GAMEZ) playoff games that decide
which National Football Conference
(NFC) team will go to the Super Bowl

NFL (EN-EFF-ELL) the National
Football League

offensive coach (AW-fen-siv KOHCH)
a coach who has responsibility for the
plays and strategies used to score points

persistent (pur-SIS-tant) unwilling to
give up

pro (PROH) a professional athlete; a
person who is paid to play a sport

recruit (ri-KROOT) to persuade an
athlete to attend a college and play for
its sports teams

running back (RUHN-ing BAK) a player
who carries the ball on running plays

sophomore (SOF-*mor*) a person in his
or her second year of high school or
college

sponsors (SPON-surz) supports people
who are doing something worthwhile,
such as charity work

vital (VYE-tuhl) very important

Bibliography

Bradley, John Ed. "Coming into His Own." *Sports Illustrated* (August 22, 2007).

King, Peter. "Philly FLASH." *Sports Illustrated* (January 28, 2002).

"1-on-1 with Donovan." *Kickoff Magazine* (Summer 2004).

www.donovanmcnabb.com

Read More

Chatlien, Michael. *Donovan McNabb.* Broomall, PA: Mason Crest (2008).

Robinson, Tom. *Donovan McNabb: Leader On and Off the Field.* Berkeley Heights, NJ: Enslow (2007).

Stewart, Mark. *The Philadelphia Eagles.* Chicago: Norwood House Press (2006).

Learn More Online

To learn more about Donovan McNabb, his foundation, and the Philadelphia Eagles, visit **www.bearportpublishing.com/FootballHeroes**

Index